Noah Had an Ark.
You Need a R.A.F.T.

Resilience **a**nd **F**lexible **T**hinking

Dr. C. Sims-Holliman

Published by Disturb the Universe, LLC

DISTURBTHEUNIVERSE, LLC

ISBN-13: 978-0-9986219-4-4

To Dad, Mom, CJ, and Astede:

Thanks for the motivation and inspiration. Oh, and for allowing me to tell your stories in my book without your permission. Love you!

For anyone who thought "it" was the end:

It's not.
If you're willing, it's only the beginning.

The Acknowledgement/Thank You/Fist Bump Section

Thank you to each of you who supported this, my latest book, by pre-ordering it early. *Throws confetti* Y'all are the real MVPs!

Aaron Bishop
Grace Christian Church
Bishop4bishop@yahoo.com

Erika Lee
P.U.R.S.E. Foundation
www.pursefoundation.org

Franchesca Warren
The Educator's Room
www.theeducatorsroom.com

Karen Weber
Weber Construction Inc
Kewebco@gmail.com

L-Mani Viney
MrViney.com
www.mrviney.com

Mariah Beall
BeatByMariahB
IG: @beatxmariahb

Saunya Williams
Saunya M. Williams, Ph.D., LLC
www.saunyawilliams.com

TiJuana Ulmer Kelley
Atlanta Public Schools
tukelley@gmail.com

Autherine Williams
Catrina Cook
Connie Byrom
Ericka Thompson
Gramisha Hernandez   **IG: @mishahernandez3**
Jasmine Jones   **IG: @jasminemdjones**
Jennifer Faniel
Jezreel Bell   **IG: @jezzy.regina**
Pamela Mount
Rachel Davis
Tkeban Jahannes
Yvette Pollard

TABLE OF CONTENTS

LET'S GET IT STARTED

Alright...so boom. Who is this book for anyway?

Well, if I said "everyone," you'd probably say, "that's awfully broad, isn't it?" And I'd completely agree with you. But the truth is, I don't know anyone who hasn't had at least one moment in their life when they **didn't** feel like all hell had broken loose. I mean, hey, stuff happens, right? And if you're one of the few who can honestly say that everything in your life has gone exactly the way you intended, congratulations! Now let me have whatever you're having.

Most of us here on earth can attest that we have found ourselves face to face with circumstances that are beyond our control. Whether it's the loss of a job, a failed relationship, a health issue, the death of a loved one, or merely a broken promise, most of us have had to figure out a response to the question, "now what?" Sometimes it's an easy fix. Other times, not so much. And it's at those times when we need to tap into a trait all of us already have. Resilience.

Resilience? Yeah. I don't think I have that.

Nope. I bet you do. You've just forgotten. **Resilience** is our ability to quickly recover from challenges or adversity, and you've been doing that since you were an infant. Don't believe me? As babies, one of the first challenges we have to overcome is our inability to walk. None of us came out of the womb knowing how but most of us learned how after falling and getting back up, more times than we can count. We were little poster children for the Chumbawamba song "Tubthumping," whose chorus says:

> *I get knocked down, but I get up again*
> *You are never gonna keep me down!*

If you've never heard of Chumbawamba, then not only do I know how old you are, you now know how old I am (and yes, I'm feeling pre-tty old right about now). But you get the point. Resilience is our ability to get knocked down but get up again, and the determination that you're never gonna be kept down.

Okay cool. Now, what's this "flexible thinking" thing you mentioned?

While resilience is a trait I believe we're all born with, flexible thinking is a trait that most of us have to learn. *Flexible Thinking*, or its formal government name Cognitive Flexibility, is best defined as our ability to adapt to new situations or overcome ways of thinking that are no longer useful. In the world of American football, this is referred to as "calling an audible," when the quarterback makes a last-minute change to a play based on what he sees the defense doing. Another way to think about it is it's our ability to think on our feet.

Most of us practice flexible thinking without even realizing it, actually. Ever been following a recipe and realize you don't have all the necessary ingredients? You might head to the grocery store or use Instacart to get what you need, but you might also adjust the recipe to use what you have on hand. You didn't stop cooking. You just adapted. And that, my friends, is what flexible thinking is, our ability to adjust our thinking.

Sounds simple enough. So, what makes you an expert on all this?

The short answer is I'm a former high school English teacher and professional learning coach with over 15 years of experience helping both students and teachers improve their best practices. I have three degrees, including a doctorate, all in the field of education, so if I can't do anything else, I can teach folks stuff. The long answer is a bit more complicated, so here's the abbreviated version.

In 2018 I survived what is commonly referred to as a "widow-maker" heart attack, a heart attack so severe that it kills most people. As a result of the trauma, I awoke from a five-day coma to find that I could no longer use my legs. While in recovery, I developed infections in my right leg and left foot that ultimately resulted in the doctors having to amputate my right leg above the knee and my left leg below it. I entered the hospital as a runner and left a partially paralyzed bilateral lower limb amputee. In the days, weeks, and months to follow, I not only had to overcome some serious challenges, but I had to adjust to my new normal also. I may not have a degree in either, but resilience and flexible thinking are two concepts I know more than a little about.

So, we're going to learn resilience and flexible thinking?

That depends. I'm going to teach you the concepts that will help you become more resilient and think more flexibly. Whether you learn anything is determined by how many of the concepts you put into practice. I can share information with you all day long but what you learn is ultimately up to you. But, because I am forever a teacher, I have left you with a little homework at the end of most chapters. It's called your **To-Do List**. This will (hopefully) help you turn your reading into doing.

Right! Anything else?

To be honest, most of what is discussed in this book won't be new to you, in theory. In many cases, it will be information that you a) already know or b) didn't realize you already knew. Nothing is at all complicated or complex even, but it might require you to come out of your comfort zone. Oh, and I'm not only a nerd I'm a corny one. So, if you come across a joke that makes you roll your eyes, go right ahead. I can't see you anyway.

Alright. You ready to get started? Let's get it!

Resilience Is...

Accepting your new reality, even if it's less good than what you had before.

Elizabeth Edwards

Resilience

So, here's the thing. Resilience isn't just one thing. It's a combination of several strategies, habits, or behaviors. In fact, based on my own life (and a little bit of research), I've discovered that resilience comprises a set of actions that I have turned into something I call **The Resilience Roadmap.** This roadmap is made of seven (7) principles that are as follows:

1. **Practice** Self-Awareness
2. **Prepare** a Positive Attitude
3. **Prioritize** Self-Care
4. **Portray** a Resilient Role Model
5. **Push Out** Fear
6. **Possess** an Inner Circle
7. **Plan** Your Outer Circle

While I've ordered them this way (because these are the steps I took to get where I am), you might not. You might only need one or a combination of more than one. Or you might decide that you need some role models to emulate before you can focus on anything else. It matters not. What does matter is that you commit to doing something.

Life by itself is interesting. Life right now is **really** interesting[1] , and chances are your comfort zone might have been obliterated. So, this is the ideal time to work on your "bounce back" game. And even if all is well with you and yours, there's never a wrong time to sharpen, or add to, your skillset. Besides, you never know

---

1 In case you're reading this at some point in the distant future it's early2020 and we're eyeball deep in the middle of the Covid-19 pandemic so yeah. "Really interesting" is the understatement of the decade so far.)

when you might have to survive a zombie apocalypse or an alien invasion. Resilience will come in handy then.

Practice Self Awareness

Practice Self Awareness

"Emotional Intelligence" is defined as "our ability to identify, assess, and control one's emotions and the emotions of others" and according to Daniel Goleman, the preeminent researcher on the topic, it is made up of four components:

- Self-Awareness

- Self-Regulation

- Self-Management

- Relationship Management

A key strategy used to develop resilience is self-awareness. And to find an excellent example of what this looks like, we just need to channel our inner Shakespeare and take this advice:

> ...*to thine own self be true.*

In other words, be authentically you. That's what self-awareness is.

The idea of authenticity seems to be gaining interest these days as people are either fighting all things fake or embracing them. I blame social media. On the one hand, it's becoming more challenging to determine what is real and what isn't in this era of "fake news," so there are now entire websites created to help us decipher between what's factual and what isn't. On the other hand, there are people (primarily teenagers and young adults), making fake social media accounts. My daughter and her friends are at the end of the Millennial Generation and the beginning of Gen Z, and they just introduced me to a new word, "Finsta," short for "fake Instagram." Young adults will sometimes use these accounts to protect who they are out of fear of being judged, ridiculed, or bullied. Other times teenagers will create these accounts to keep their parents "out of their business." I have never been so happy to be officially old.

Self-awareness is all about understanding and embracing, who we are, what we value, and what we believe. It also allows us to understand better how other people perceive us. The quote from earlier, the one from Shakespeare's *Hamlet,* is incomplete. The full quote is as follows:

This above all: to thine own self be true. And it must follow, as the day does the night, **thou canst not then be false to any man.**

When we are true to ourselves, people can't misinterpret or misrepresent who we are to others. This doesn't mean that they won't. What it **does** mean is that people who have encountered you will know whether or not what is being said about you is accurate. For example, anyone who knows me knows that I love my kids, and after teaching for over 15 years, I have a lot of them. You can look at my social posts or their social media posts and see all the times I brag about their accomplishments. I cheer them on just like they were my biological children. So, if anyone were to say that I spoke disparagingly about them or said I hated them, no one would believe it. I always try to make sure that the external me aligns with the internal me. Practicing self-awareness means being able to evaluate ourselves objectively and take an honest look at who we are.

Another way that we practice self-awareness is by overcoming challenges. We are our most authentic selves when all hell is breaking loose. If you've ever tried to maintain your composure when someone has ticked you off, then you know exactly what I mean. A mild example is when we're in traffic. The real me comes out every time someone cuts me off without regard to my safety. The past me would have hurled every expletive I knew, but all it takes is for this to happen one time in the car with a young child who repeats everything you say, and you quickly begin to reevaluate your behavior.

Make no mistake, possessing self-awareness takes practice. But, there are a few ways we can improve in this area and thereby make ourselves more resilient.

The To-Do List

1. **Recognize our strengths and weakness:** By knowing what we're good at and what we need to work on, we can focus on improvements in the areas of concern.
2. **Self-reflect:** Thinking about our actions, decisions, responses to stressors, etc. is an excellent way to address any issues that might have gone unnoticed.
3. **Ask for feedback:** When we don't have an accurate view of ourselves, we must get honest feedback from someone we trust.
4. **Contemplate the consequences:** For any decision we make, we should provide at least two reasons why we should pursue it. This way, we can better understand our rationale and ensure we're choosing the best possible option for the best possible reason.
5. **Watch what we say:** Be conscious of the things we tell ourselves. As we'll discover later in the book, what we say to ourselves builds the houses we eventually live in.

Prepare A Positive Attitude

Prepare a Positive Attitude

Since we've already established that resilience is our ability to recover quickly from setbacks and difficulties mentally, we understand that much of our capacity for recovery comes from what goes on inside of our heads. It's what we say to ourselves when no one else is around. But the truth is, sometimes this is much easier to say than it is to do, especially when everything around us is falling apart.

As a former high school English teacher, I had the pleasure of teaching 9th Grade. Yes. I said, "pleasure" because it was just that. Was it easy? A lot of times, no. It wasn't. But I believed, and still believe, that teaching freshman is the best job in the building. I had the privilege of watching my students transform over four years. Many of them came to me saddled with all types of insecurities and worries, most of which I had to help them overcome before they could move forward. One of the most pervasive was their thinking around failure, and because we live in a culture that tells us that failure is the opposite of success, they were truly perplexed when I told them, "failure is actually a part of success."

If you've never heard this before now, you might be giving me "The Look." This is the face you make when someone tells you something so ridiculous you can't help but think they must be lying. I know this because that's the same look I gave my father the first time he said it to me, right after I flunked out of my first semester of college.

Granted, he didn't say it quite like that. What he actually said was,

Experience is the gift you only receive after you've failed.

It was at that moment, I knew. My father was insane.

And it would take me many more years before I fully understood what he meant.

If you don't ever fail at anything, you don't ever learn anything.

But I also discovered that my father was a pretty brilliant man despite being the one I argued with the most.

For an excellent example of the point my father was trying to make, we have to look no further than Michael Jordan, arguably one of the greatest basketball players to have ever lived. He also didn't make his high school varsity basketball team the first time he tried out. What if he had been so discouraged that he never tried out again? What if he had never used his spot on the JV team to hone his skills? What if he had chosen defeat instead of failure? Well, Nike wouldn't have made $2.86 billion off of Jordan's brand in 2018, and we would have never had the cinematic genius that is *Space Jam,* and we all know what a travesty that would be.

At this point, the last question I asked might give you pause. What did I mean when I said that Jordan could have chosen defeat instead of failure? Here goes my father being brilliant again.

Defeat is falling down and choosing to stay there.
Failure is falling down and choosing not to.

(I'm telling you. My next book might just be about my dad.)

Although we often use "defeat" and "failure" interchangeably (someone who is defeated has failed and someone who has failed has been defeated), I submit to you the most significant difference between the two is pretty simple. Choosing failure means we can see the positive side of a thing while defeat means we can't. Again, it's all about the words we speak to ourselves.

So, what are some practical ways we can possess a positive attitude? On the next page are my Top 5

The To-Do List

1) **Choose to Be Happy:** Some situations warrant sadness or anger, but not all of them do.

2) **Stop Complaining:** Everything isn't bad. Some things may be. Heck, a lot of stuff may be, but not everything. Find the good stuff.

3) **Do Something Nice for Someone:** And that someone can be someone else or that someone can be you, although I find my attitude improves more when I do something nice for someone else.

4) **Practice Being Grateful:** There are a million reasons why whatever you're dealing with could have been worse. Be appreciative of what you have.

5) **Uplift the People Around You:** One of the best ways I've found to stay positive is by being a source of encouragement to the people around me. One kind word can go a long way.

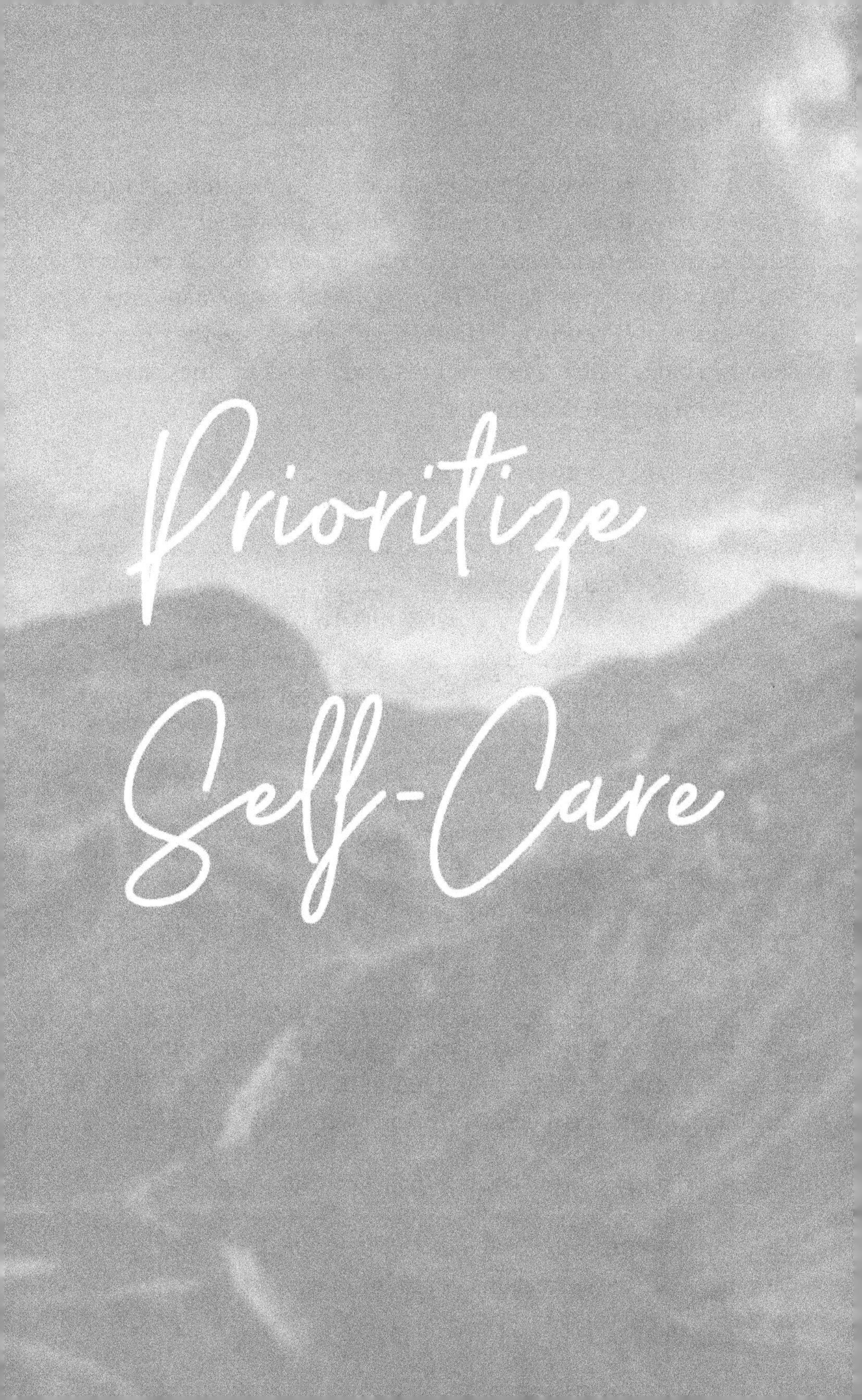
Prioritize
Self-Care

Prioritize Self Care

One of the funniest shows of all time, in my opinion, is *Parks and Recreation*. If you're unfamiliar with the show, but you are familiar with *The Office*, well, it's what *The Office* would be if it were located in the parks and recreation office of a small midwestern town. If you're not familiar with either one, they're great shows to binge watch when you're at home sick or stuck in a snowstorm or under quarantine.

In Season Four, two characters named Tom and Donna celebrate their favorite day of October 13. What makes this day so special? Simple. October 13 is Annual "Treat Yo Self" Day. Never heard of it? Not surprising, unless you're familiar with the show. But "Treat You Self" Day is the day that Tom and Donna set aside every year to, well, treat themselves. Whatever they feel like doing that's going to make them happy or feel good, that's what they do.

Want a banana split? Treat Yo Self!
Really like that cashmere sweater? Treat You Self!
Want a massage? Treat Yo Self!
Want to curse somebody out? Take a nap first and then...
TREAT YO SELF!

While the writers made up this day for the show, the idea is a great one. If two fictional characters can decide that on the same day each year that they're going to put themselves first and do all the things that make them happy, then why can't we?

Because we're not fictional characters, and we have things to do.

These are both true.
But, that's not the correct answer to the question.

The correct answer to the question is whatever reason you came up with in your head when I posed the question. Here are a few I came up with:

I have too much work to do.
I can't take any time off.
The kids have (whatever the kids have).
I have to (whatever it is that you have to do).
I don't need any time off. I'm fine.

Any of those sound familiar?

But here's the truth, and I need you to listen very carefully; you can't recover from an issue or set back if you **don't** take the time to "treat yo self."

In 2016, I was placed on medical leave from my position as a teacher. Physically I wasn't doing well, and emotionally I was exhausted. When I went to the doctor, I was there because I had a cough I couldn't shake. I figured he'd just fuss at me like he did every time I waited too late to see him, prescribe some medicine, and send me on my way. This time was different. He walked into the exam room, took one look at me, and said, "What in the world is going on with you?" I looked as bad as I felt.

He looked at my blood pressure, looked back at my chart, then looked at me.

"That's it," he said. "I'm sending you home for two months."

I began to protest, using almost all of the reasons listed on the previous page. And he listened. And nodded his head.

And he made me call my principal from his office and tell her I wouldn't be at work for the next two months.

Thankfully, I had a very understanding principal who, interestingly enough, not only agreed with my doctor's decision but said, "it's about time you took a break."

It was a conspiracy.

And one I was thankful for because I didn't know how to stop. See, I have the quintessential Type A personality. I am a perfectionist and a workaholic. The fact that this day hadn't happened sooner was a miracle. And just so I can make it very clear how serious of a workaholic I was, I was out for two months and didn't lose one day of pay. Truthfully, I could've stayed out for almost six months because that's how much sick time I'd accrued. I went to work even when I was ill, and when I wasn't at work, I was working from home **on** work **for** work.

Here in Metro Atlanta, where I live, a local news station whose tag line is, "Dedicated. Determined. Dependable." That was me. If something needed to be taken care of, I would make sure it got taken care of. Except, the most crucial thing that needed to be taken care of was me, and I wasn't doing that at all. I thought I was doing an excellent job of hiding it. On the surface, I had it all together. But my doctor knew better. So, when I lost a student in a car accident, got behind in my grading, started struggling to keep up with my graduate schoolwork, and had a complete meltdown, no one was surprised except me.

There is an adage that says,

You can't pour from an empty cup,

which simply means you can't give what you don't have. We can't be resilient if we're worn out or sick from taking care of everything and everyone else. We need every bit of our strength and sanity to tackle obstacles as they come, so we have to become good at taking care of ourselves first. It took my getting very sick before I understood that self-care isn't selfish, and you don't get any extra brownie points for pushing yourself over the edge. So, TREAT YO SELF! Here are a few ideas to try:

The To-Do List

1) **Get some sleep:** Make getting a good night's sleep tops on your priority list.

2) **Eat Healthy:** While the double espresso and glazed doughnut might help you get through your morning, what you eat contributes to how you feel.

3) **"No" is a complete sentence:** You don't need to say "yes" to others until you've said "yes" to yourself. Make yourself your #1 priority.

4) **Take a vacation:** Go away, and while you're there, only do what you want to do, even if that's nothing.

5) **Spend time outside:** If a vacation isn't feasible, go for a walk in the park, or to the store, or zoo, or anywhere that isn't confined by four walls and a roof.

6) **Schedule a self-care day:** You can celebrate with Tom and Donna on October 13, or you can pick another day, but whatever you do, make time once a month if you can to... you already know what to say.

Portray A
PPM

Portray a Resilient Role Model

When we are young, we often have people that we look up to. Sports figures, superheroes, historical figures, family members, celebrities can all fall into this category. Our dreams and aspirations become both believable and achievable when we can look to someone else who has done what we want to do. Having a role model lets us know that not only **can** it be done but that it's already **been** done, which means it can be done again by us.

Whether in our personal or professional lives, we often need the reassurance of seeing someone else accomplish great things to inspire and encourage us to do the same. The same is true when we are trying to increase our resiliency. To become more resilient, it often helps to look to someone who has experienced a challenging situation and made it through to the other side. So, in this section, I'm going to share with you the stories of five people who have persevered through some trying situations despite the hardships they faced. Hopefully, you'll find a resilient role model to look up to.

1) Oprah Winfrey: Television and Media Mogul

Look on most lists about resilient people, and you are sure to find Oprah Winfrey among them. The story of her life is one that, by all indications, should've never turned out the way it has. Her childhood was marred with trauma, including finding herself pregnant at 15 and then losing the baby. Her television career almost didn't happen when she was publicly fired from her first job as a television anchor because she was "too emotionally invested in her stories." Now, she is one of the world's wealthiest women, with a net worth standing at close to $3 billion.

2) Steven Spielberg: Director

The University of Southern California School of Cinematic Arts (USC Film School) is widely considered one of the best film schools in the United States, if not the world. Ron Howard *(Apollo 13)*, George Lucas *(Star Wars)*, John Singleton *(Boyz n the Hood)*, Robert Zemeckis *(Forest Gump)*, and Craig Zisk *(Parks and Recreation)* can all count themselves as alumni of this prestigious institution. The one famous person who cannot is Steven Spielberg. The director of *E.T.*, *Jaws, Close Encounters,* all of the movies in the *Jurassic Park* series, and countless others was rejected three times. His films' unprecedented success has earned him the title of one of the top five richest movie directors globally, with a net worth of approximately $3.7 billion.

3) J.K. Rowling: Author

If Oprah Winfrey's name is found on most lists about overcoming adversity, author J.K. Rowling is almost certainly on there as well. Before her wildly successful books about a young wizard made her a multi-millionaire, Rowling was an impoverished single mother battling depression and unemployment. It took several rejections before she sold her first book *Harry Potter and the Philosopher's Stone,* for around $4,000.

Now, the *Potter Series* are among the most recognizable books and movies in the world and have netted Rowling over $1 billion.

4) Chris Gardner: Businessman

This name might not sound familiar to you, but it should. If you were into movies around 2006, then you will recall a film starring Will Smith called *The Pursuit of Happyness* about a struggling single father determined to make a better life for him and his son. Eventually, he becomes a stockbroker and starts his brokerage firm. And while Will Smith did an excellent job in this role, he wasn't playing a fictional character. He was retelling Chris Gardner's life, one that has resulted in him becoming a multi-millionaire.

5) Robert Kiyosaki, Businessman

Here is another name that might not sound familiar to you unless you're one of the 28 million people worldwide who have read, learned, and been inspired by any of the books in the *Rich Dad Poor Dad* series. Between the ages of 30-50, Kiyosaki started two different businesses, both of which ended up bankrupt, and a third that he eventually sold. It wasn't until he was 50 that he wrote the book for which he is now famous, a book that has been translated into 51 different languages and has made him a multi-millionaire.

Push Out Fear

Push Out Fear

Answer: Butterflies.
Question: What are the things my child is afraid of?

When my daughter was in kindergarten, she and her classmates visited a botanical garden. It was a beautiful spring day, and she was doing what all the other five-year-olds were doing, running and walking on the path that wove its way through the flora and fauna. At the center of the garden was the butterfly habitat, a beautiful all-glass building with an aromatic array of flowers. The children followed their teacher inside, and almost immediately, the butterflies started doing what they do, fly. Unfortunately for my daughter, the butterflies **really** liked her, and it seemed like every butterfly in the enclosure made a collective decision to land on her all at the same time. She had butterflies on her arms, in her hair, and on her back. It looked like something straight out of a horror movie. My poor little girl started crying and flailing and running until she was out of the enclosure, and then one of her teachers had to chase after her because she was going to get as far away as she possibly could. My daughter is 23 years old now, and butterflies still make her skin crawl. At least she's no longer running away from them. Wanna know what she's **not** afraid of?

Snakes. Worms. Bugs. Roller Coasters.

You know, things she probably **should** be afraid of.

But my kid is different, like her mother.

So, I guess since I shared my daughter's fear with you, I should also share mine. I have usual fears. Snakes, worms, bugs, unicorns, and dragons. Okay. I'm not afraid of unicorns and dragons anymore, but both of them kept me up at night when I was a child. I was scared they were under my bed, conspiring to get me. Mind you, I had no idea what they would do if they actually got me, but I didn't want to find out. And where did my fear of these two mythical creatures come from? One place and one place only.

Television.

I'm not sure what was going on in my six- or seven-year-old mind, but it was the 70s, and the movie *The Last Unicorn* and the television special *Puff the Magic Dragon* gave me nightmares. It's only been recently that I've been able to watch *The Last Unicorn* without getting the willies because I figured there wasn't a good reason for a 47-year old woman to be afraid of unicorns. Still not my favorite mythical creature, but they no longer give me the willies. Dragons are cool, though.

So, what does any of this have to do with developing resilience? One meaningful way to become more resilient is to face our fears and then leave them behind. This is especially important if what we are afraid of falls into the category of "irrational." Holding on to this type of fear is unhealthy and can keep us from moving forward. For example, I grew up terrified of public speaking, a widespread fear among many people. But, my anxiety was so intense, I used to get physically ill. Even now, when I have to speak in front of people, I still get a little queasy in the stomach, but I've been speaking publicly now for at least 25 years. Had I never faced this fear, I would have never been able to become a teacher. I would have never been able to speak at conferences or coach groups of teachers. I'd have missed out on some of the best moments of my life thus far.

We understand that some fear is healthy. It was fear that told our prehistoric ancestors to run from the big furry thing with the claws and teeth. It's healthy fear that helps keep us safe when we are in a dangerous environment. That's where we get our "fight or flight" reactions from. But any fear that keeps us from living our absolute best lives is something we have to face. Here are two quotes for you to think about:

Fear defeats more people than any other one thing in the world.
Ralph Waldo Emerson

Do the thing you fear to do and keep on doing…that is the quickest and surest way ever yet discovered to conquer fear.
Dale Carnegie

Usually, what we are afraid of is something that we don't feel confident in. I didn't feel confident speaking in public, so I was fearful of it. Fear is also present when we get caught in the "what-if" cycle. We've all been stuck here, especially when we are facing the unknown. We can paralyze ourselves thinking about all the bad things that **could** happen, so we avoid dealing with whatever it is.

Back in the early 2000s, there was a show that aired called *Fear Factor*. The show's premise was that contestants would win money for doing things that would normally scare them. Most of what they were asked to do were either extreme (lying in a coffin while tarantulas are poured all over them) or disgusting (I'm not going to give you an example). The show only lasted one season, but the idea behind it is not unfamiliar. The creators were doing a sensationalized version of "exposure therapy," where people are forced to face their fears by being exposed to what they are afraid of. We can do this for ourselves (without tarantulas and coffins) by merely changing the way we respond to our fear.

When we face a scary situation, our first reaction is to allow fear to creep in. But, here are some ways we can meet our fears so we can leave them behind.

The To-Do List

1) **Speak to It:** At the moment when anxiety shows up, stop, and address it. I know this may sound strange, but we need to speak to our fear. We need to ask it what it wants. What is it trying to get us to avoid? If it's trying to keep us out of a dangerous situation (like walking off a curb into oncoming traffic), we need to listen. If it's trying to keep us from doing something that can be for our benefit, we need to dig a little deeper and figure out why.

2) **Reframe It (Part A):** As we've already discussed, getting caught in the "what-if" cycle can be debilitating. Instead of worrying about what might happen, we can ask, "what's the worst that could happen?" This allows us to filter through all those worst-case scenarios and, hopefully, see that there's no outcome that we can't reasonably handle, with or without help.

3) **Reframe It (Part B):** Instead of asking, "what's the worst that could happen," we can ask, "what's the best that could happen?" By reframing it, you move the "what if" cycle from being fear-based to being reward-based.

4) **Do It Scared:** Referring back to the quote by Daniel Carnegie, sometimes the best way to conquer fear is to do the thing we fear. Whether our fear disappears while doing the thing or it simply diminishes, eventually, what we fear will no longer frighten us. As one of my favorite quotes says, "Do the scary thing and get scared later."

5) **Breathe Slowly:** This sounds really simple, I know, but it works. Usually, when we are afraid, we start to breathe more rapidly, leading to hyperventilation. Hyperventilating can cause us to become more anxious because we can't catch our breath, which just leads to more

fear. When we are afraid, we need to focus on regulating our breathing by breathing in for three or four seconds, holding our breath for three or four seconds, and then exhaling in three or four seconds. Once we've calmed down, we can then reason about what we need to do.

Possess an Inner Circle

Possess an Inner Circle

In 2019, there seemed to have been a social media movement that encouraged people to protect their peace by any means necessary. Facebook, Instagram, and Twitter were replete with posts about unfriending, unfollowing, and disconnecting from people who were toxic to our mental, physical, spiritual, or emotional well-being. One of my favorites said:

I will unfriend, uncousin, unco-worker-unfollow, unfamily a draining soul real quick.

I cannot begin to explain the degree to which I want to find whoever came up with this statement so I can hug them.

One of the biggest enemies to self-resilience is having people who aren't good for us in our lives. Those who never have anything nice to say about us (or anyone else for that matter) are not people who need to be occupying space in our lives. It is challenging to be an overcomer when we have a person, or people, continually trying to tear us down. That's why we have to be very selective about who we allow ourselves to be accessible to.

Before we know who we need to disassociate with, we need to first establish which types of friends we have in our lives. Bishop TD Jakes, in his book *Destiny,* identifies three types:

1) **Confidants:** People who are for us for the long haul; they love us unconditionally.
2) **Constituents:** People who are not into us; they are simply into what we stand for.

3) **Comrades:** People who aren't for us or what we stand for; they are just against what we are against.

Clearly, the people in category one are those we should keep. These are the people I refer to as "The Crew." These people will cry with us and for us, laugh with us and for us and, if necessary, fight with us and for us. These are the people who will speak on our behalf if someone is trying to talk negatively about us. But what about two and three? That depends. If we take on a significant challenge, both might prove useful assets, but if things don't go the way we planned, either one could quickly turn into a liability.

Now that we've looked at the three types of friends, we need to look at the various kinds of non-friends. The fact that that there are more categories of non-friends than there are friends should tell you something. We're not going to look at all of them, but here are four we all have probably encountered[2]:

1) **Toxic:** This person gives the impression of providing support but actively works to undermine our efforts
2) **Counterfeit:** This is the "fake friend," the one who gives the impression of being a friend but isn't someone who can be trusted.
3) **Fair-Weather:** This person disappears during a time of need but will return once a lousy time or situation passes.
4) **Spiteful:** Affectionately referred to as "the hater," this person is jealous of our efforts to achieve.

[2] Young, S L. "Friendship Categories and Classifications: What's Your Friend's Type?" *Huffington Post*, 23 Mar. 2015, https://www.huffpost.com/entry/friendship-categories-and-classification_b_6511362.

"Possess an Inner Circle" can fit into the section on "Self-Care," but I wanted us to address it separately because who we are in a relationship with can make or break us, especially when we are trying to climb our way out of an emotional hole. A piece of advice I give out often is:

Not everyone who is with you is for you.

I need you to pause and read that one more time.

Let it sink in.

Not everyone who is in your circle should be. A young man I met when I was still teaching put it like this:

There are people in your circle who don't like you. They aren't there to support you. They're there so when you become successful, they can say they know you.

To be clear, there is a difference between our "friend" friends and our "work" friends or acquaintances. Our "friend" friends are the people around us when we are at our best and there when we're at our worst. Regardless of what happens in our lives, they're not going anywhere. These are also people who we can vent to and know that it's not going to go beyond the two of us. It's a matter of trust, and when we're working on becoming more resilient, we need to be around people we can trust.

The biggest takeaway I want you to have from this is this: **Check Your Circle**. And after you check your circle, push out anyone who doesn't have your best interest at heart. Here are a few quotes to help you remember. To keep them in the forefront of your mind, write them on index cards and tape them to your mirror. Make it the lock screen on your phone. Write them on sticky notes and put them in your car. Do whatever you have to do so you don't forget.

1) *Everyone doesn't deserve a front-row seat to your life.*
2) *Getting unfriended can be a blessing.*
3) *It's a privilege to have access to me in any capacity.*
4) *A real friend is one who walks in when others walk out*
   -Walter Winchell
5) *Don't make friends who are comfortable to be with. Make friends who will force you to level up.*
   -Thomas J. Watson
6) *A friend is someone who understands your past, believes in your future, and accepts you just the way you are.*
7) *What you do not want done to yourself, do not do to others.*
   -Confucius
8) *No person is your friend who demands your silence or denies your right to grow.* **-Alice Walker**
9) *Lots of people want to ride with you in the limo, but what you want is someone who will take the bus with you when the limo breaks down.* **Oprah Winfrey**
10) *If you make friends with yourself, you will never be alone.*
    -Maxwell Maltz

Plan Your Outer Circle

Plan Your Outer Circle

When I began my career as a teacher, I was one of those new teachers who chose the profession so I could change the world. I was full of idealism and creativity but utterly oblivious to how hard being a world changer was going to be. In my first year, I strived to be the best for my students. I wanted their parents to know that I was committed to the education of their children. I wanted my department chair and my principal to believe that they had made an excellent choice when they decided to hire me. I wanted my colleagues to see me as a trusted and dependable team member. I was channeling my inner Whitney Houston daily:

I believe the children are our future
Teach them well and let them lead the way
Show them all the beauty they possess inside
Give them a sense of pride to make it easier
Let the children's laughter remind us how we used to be

(Go ahead and sing. I don't mind one bit.)

I did everything I knew to do, including taking home stacks of work to grade every day.

At the end of every six weeks, students were given a progress report to bring home to their parents. Before sending them out, we would have a department meeting to complete a "grade book audit." A "grade book audit" is when our department chair checked to ensure we had an appropriate number of graded assignments. At the end of six weeks, most

teachers in my department had between 10 and 12, approximately two graded assignments per week. I, on the other hand, had 36. I was grading homework assignments, tests, quizzes, classwork, essays, etc. If it had a student's name on it, I was giving it a grade.

I remember when my colleagues found out how many grades I had, and they laughed for a full two minutes. I was immediately embarrassed and started gathering up my things so I could make a quick exit. Right then, our department's matriarch (she'd been teaching for 30 years by the time I arrived) placed her hand on my shoulder.

"Well, now we know why you go home every day looking like a bag lady. Ma'am, you do NOT need to put everything in the grade book." I looked up at her with tears welling up in my eyes and said,

"Huh? I don't?" The rest of my colleagues laughed again.

"Girl, no!" They then explained why and gave me other ways to determine my students' progress without burying myself in paper. I immediately felt relieved.

As I was leaving to go home, our matriarch walked me to my car and said,

"Don't you ever go home carrying all those bags of work again. Maybe on the weekend but not every day and not every weekend."

I followed that advice for the entire 15 years I spent in education, and it's advice I now pass on to the teachers I work with.

Unfortunately, some teachers don't have the type of support I had as a first-year teacher. The situation with my grades could have turned into something very stressful, and discouraging had I not had these people in my professional network.

When we're in a new environment, or even if we're in an old one, having colleagues, constituents, or comrades who are in our corner can make us more resilient. One reason is that we know we have people who are going to help guide us and offer us advice so we can tackle whatever challenges come our way.

The other benefit of having a supportive network is that you're a part of someone else's supportive network too. You can develop resiliency by sharing with others how you conquered your issues. One of the reasons I moved from teaching students in the classroom to coaching other teachers is so I could be for someone else what my network was for me. When we share our stories of triumph with others, we offer hope and let them know that they aren't alone in their mishaps, missteps, or mistakes.

No man (or woman) is an island.

We shouldn't have to go through anything alone, especially if we are in an environment where people have traveled the same road we are currently traveling on.

Sadly, sometimes our work environments aren't the best places to secure a supportive network. If this is true for you, look to other locations or organizations. Joining religious groups, civic organizations, fraternities, sororities, extramural sports clubs, hobby-related groups, business organizations, etc. are great ways to cultivate a supportive network. And by doing so, we put ourselves in the position of having people who can help us fly after we fall.

Flexible Thinking

We cannot solve our problems with the same thinking we used when we created them.

Albert Einstein

Flexible Thinking

In the same way that resilience isn't just one concept, *cognitive flexibility* or **flexible thinking** isn't either. As we've already established, flexible thinking is our ability to think on our feet, to shift or pivot so we can move forward. If you've ever had a problem you couldn't find the solution for, you might need some help with your flexible thinking. No worries. I got you covered.

Since this book is called *Noah Had an Ark. You Need a Raft,* flexible thinking concepts are acronyms that spell out S.A.I.L. and W.I.N.D. I mean, you need a sail and some wind if you want your raft to move, right? So, the concepts are as follows:

Slay the Sacred Cow

Allow for Multiple Answers

Imagineer Solutions

Learn to Take Risks

Widen Your Perspective

Interrupt the Idea

Neutralize Your Thoughts

Destroy the Box

I must confess that these chapters are longer than those in the Resilience section, and that's because you didn't really need to be taught how to be resilient. You just needed a few reminders. On the other hand, Flexible Thinking is a skill that requires practice, and for many of us, it's not one that we've ever learned or learned well. So take your time here. There's no need to rush, and I would actually suggest that you don't. Much of flexible thinking challenges you to be willing to change your mindset. If you're not ready to do that, then leave this section until you are.

And since I brought up mindset, let me give you two definitions to think about. Based on research done by Stanford psychologist Carol Dweck, there are two types, a **fixed mindset,** and a **growth mindset**. A *fixed mindset* says, "my qualities are fixed traits that can't be improved upon or changed." You believe that either you're good at something or bad at something, and that's that. It's all black and white with absolutely no shades of grey. A *growth mindset* says, "I'm not good at this now, so what can I do to get better?" You see failure as an invitation to try something else, and it propels you to stretch your existing abilities. So, which one do you possess? Think about it, and if you're ready, I'll see you on the next page.

Slay the Sacred Cow

Slay the Sacred Cow

I know in other cultures, cows are sacred. Here in the South (Georgia, to be exact), cows are a protected species, so says Chik-Fil-A (Eat Mor Chikin y'all). But that's not what this section is about. **This** section is about dispelling the myth that just because it's been done one way, that's the only way it should ever be done.

What exactly is a "Sacred Cow" anyway?

Glad you asked. A "sacred cow" is,

1) Someone or something that is considered to have a status that allows it to avoid any criticism or questioning;

2) Something that is considered above reproach or immune to negative criticism, it is an allusion to cows' sacred status in the Hindu religion.

3) Something that is regarded by some people with such respect and veneration that they do not like it being criticized by anyone in any way.

These are all definitions that can be easily found by doing a Google search (that's what I did). But I want to add a fourth definition to the list:

4) **Any idea, concept, or rule you refuse to give up because you're stubborn and don't like change.**

Yup. That part

If you're of the school of thought that says, "this is the way it's been done, and this is the way it should always be done," go ahead and quit right now because you're not ever going to accomplish anything. What's the definition of "insanity" again?

Doing the same thing over and over expecting different results.

Now before you get angry, I hear you. What if what you've been doing has been working? Well, if you weren't looking for a more excellent way, then I doubt you'd be reading this book. But, even if you **aren't** looking for a more excellent way and you have no plans to slay anything (except maybe your outfit), may I submit to you the Gospel According to Shuri:

"Just because something works doesn't mean it can't be improved."

Now, suppose you're not a bonified Marvel nerd and are unfamiliar with the MCU (Marvel Cinematic Universe), or you completely missed the behemoth of a movie that was The Black Panther. In that case, you don't know who Shuri is. Shuri is the younger sister of T'Challa, aka The Black Panther, and she is a technological genius. She is also, as far as I'm concerned, the ultimate Sacred Cow Slayer (Not to be confused with the King Slayer of *Game of Thrones* fame, but I digress). Look what she says again,

"Just because something works doesn't mean it can't be improved."

This statement applies to her brother as much as it applies to us. Something can have worked for millennia, but that doesn't mean that it can't be made better. A perfect example is telephones, specifically landlines. Do landlines still work? Yup. Are they still useful? Yup. Would you give up your cell phone for just a landline? Probably not.

If we are to embrace this first concept of Flexible Thinking, we have to be, well, flexible in our thinking. We have to stop holding on to things that are no longer useful to us, EVEN IF THEY STILL WORK, so that we can move forward. I mean, typewriters still work but do you really think I'm getting ready to trade in my tablet, or heck even my cell phone, for a typewriter just because it works? Right. Nope.

The key to "slaying the sacred cow" is this: Stop doing things because they're familiar and comfortable and decide to do somethings differently. There are countless real-world examples of what happens when you are resistant to change. Here are a few to consider:

Blockbuster (1985-2010)

In the 80s and 90s, Blockbuster stores were the go-to location for video rentals. Before we were "Netflix and Chilling," we were "Making it a Blockbuster night."

In 2000, the now-ubiquitous Netflix owners approached Blockbuster with an offer they shouldn't have refused. They offered to sell the company to Blockbuster for $50 million. The CEO turned it down because he didn't see the value of online movies, which, at the time, were losing money. Besides,

Blockbuster was the leader in the video rental business, so why change?

In 2010, Blockbuster declared bankruptcy, and the only place you can find a Blockbuster card now is in a museum or probably in a junk drawer at my parents' house. And Netflix? As of 2018, Netflix had over 250 million subscribers worldwide and annual revenue of $15.79 billion.

Kodak (1888-2012)

Those of us of a certain age remember not only taking pictures with Kodak film but sending it off to our local drug store to have it developed. For over 100 years, Kodak was the market leader in the photography industry until it wasn't. In 1975, Kodak created the first digital camera but didn't follow through with it out of fear of destroying their film business. It was ultimately destroyed anyway when digital photography took over. By the time they had the ultimate "facepalm" moment, it was too late. Their rivals saw the market changing and took over what Kodak had started.

MySpace (2003-2008)

I never got into MySpace. But I know lots of Millennials who did. Founded in 2003, MySpace was the social media darling when Mark Zuckerberg offered to sell Facebook to it in 2005 for $75 million. The CEO at the time turned the offer down. Whereas MySpace was created to connect people primarily through music, Good 'ol Zuck recognized that people wanted to communicate in more ways than just one. So, he made a platform to connect with whomever we chose through family, friends, hobbies, political views, **and** music. MySpace couldn't, or wouldn't, adapt, and now the juggernaut that is Facebook has taken over the world.

Notice any similarities between these three companies? Whether it was arrogance, stubbornness, fear, or willful ignorance, each of these companies failed because they refused to change. They were at the top of their respective industries and couldn't see the need to do anything differently, so they didn't. And now, we talk about them in the past tense instead of the present. How will we be talking about you?

Allow for Multiple Answers

Allow for Multiple Answers

As a former teacher, I hear lots of stories from many kids about what their teachers did or didn't do to them or for them.

"She wouldn't let me be the line leader!"
"I asked him if I could turn it in late, and he said 'no!'"
"She doesn't even like me, though!"

So, I wasn't surprised when one of my students came to me with her little sister's situation.

"Mrs. Holliman, you need to go and speak to my little sister's teacher."
"Why would I need to do that?"
"Because she marked one of the answers to her questions wrong when it was right!"
"And I'm supposed to help how?"
"Explain to her what you teach us, that there's no such thing as a right or wrong answer, just want you can prove and what you can't!" (We'll get back to this idea in a moment)
"Well…not everyone believes that, so I probably shouldn't be going into someone else's classroom telling them how to teach."
"But you **should** because her teacher is wrong."

Insert deep sigh and eye roll here

"Okay. Why is the teacher with the degree, and the certification, and the years of experience teaching, wrong?"
" Because she is. Look."

My student gave me the paper, and this was the question:

Michael had a dozen doughnuts. After visiting with his friends, he had 4 doughnuts remaining. Write the equation and explain what happened.

Here is what my student's little sister wrote:

$$12 = \text{total doughnuts}$$
$$2 = \text{total friends}$$
$$12/2 = 6 \text{ for each friend}$$
$$6 - 2 = 4 \text{ (Michael wanted 2 doughnuts too)}$$

Her equation was:

$$(12/2) - 2 = 4$$

Now, I'm no math genius, but I'm **pretty** sure this is a correct answer to the question she was asked. But the teacher had it marked wrong. I asked my student if her sister had asked the teacher why it was mismarked.

"Yup. She told her that wasn't the answer she was looking for."

"What's her teacher's name? I'll find her number…"

So…let me start from the beginning.

For almost 15 years, I had the pleasure of being a high school English teacher, 9th Grade, to be exact, and one of the things that frustrated me most was that my students didn't know how to think. I know. You're saying, "how can kids not know how to think?" Or, if you've you ever had a 9th grader living in your house, you might be nodding your head in agreement. Either way, my students were coming to me conditioned only to supply the answers their teachers wanted. And then they met me, and our first few classes would go a little something like this:

"Okay, class. The author of this passage said *(whatever the author said)*. What do you think he meant?"

Blank stares
60 seconds pass

"Anyone have any ideas? Anyone?"

More blank stares
Silence
60 more seconds pass

"Aren't you going to tell us? I mean, what's the right answer?"

"I don't know. You tell me."

Even more blank stares
More silence
Eye rolls

"What do you mean, 'tell you?' Don't you know? Aren't you the teacher?"

"Yup and yup."

An abundance of blank stares
Even more silence
Multiple eye rolls and grumbling

After many rounds of this, I quickly realized that not only were they conditioned to give the answers their teachers wanted, they'd been taught that there was only ever one correct answer. Consequently, only one way for something to be done. (Sound at all familiar to you?) I also realized that they were hesitant to take the leap and provide whatever answer they thought was correct because they were terrified of being wrong. They didn't want to fail.

Failure is an interesting concept, by the way. What constitutes failure depends on who you ask. Think about it. Earning a "C" on a paper might be considered a failure for a student used to getting straight "A's." But it might feel like an "A" for a student used to getting "F's." Somehow, they had been taught that if their answer didn't match the teacher's explanation, it was wrong. I blame the whole standardized testing climate for this, but the truth is, most of us have been conditioned to only look for one answer to something.

And therein lies the problem.

Let's go back to for a moment:

> *There is no such thing as a right or wrong answer.*
> *Simply what you can prove and what you can't.*

Now, I'm not going to say that I was a brilliant teacher all the time, but when I got something right, I got it right.

Once I shared this sentiment with the class, I then threw another "Hollimanism" at them for good measure.

"And perchance, you **do** get an answer 'wrong' just keep trying until you come up with one that isn't."

Blank stares
Eye blinks
Silence

And then...

One hand raised. Then two. Then a class full. So, what happened? What **happened** was I permitted them to fail. By allowing them to fail, I also gave them the freedom to try, and when they realized that **their** answer might not to be **my** answer, but it could still be a **right** answer, well, let's just say they never looked at responding to questions the same way again.

I realize my philosophy about tackling questions or problems might sound a bit off-putting to you. I know it did to my colleagues because my students would go to their other classes and give their teachers fits. (Tee hee.) But the truth is I am challenging the status quo *on purpose*. Remember, this is the section on developing Flexible Thinking, and one way to

think flexibly is to throw a monkey wrench into our belief systems.

One belief system that surely needs to be pummeled by a whole host of monkeys with wrenches is the one that says

there can only be one correct answer to a question or problem. And how do we that? It's quite simple, actually. We start first by swapping out "the" with "a" or "an."

Let's look back at the question my student's sister was given:

Michael had a dozen doughnuts. After visiting with his friends, he had 4 doughnuts remaining. Write the equation and explain what happened.

The way this is written suggests, there is only one acceptable answer to the problem, and we know that because of the word "the."

> *Write **the** equation and explain what happened.*

Now, what does the problem look like if we swap the "the" with "an?"

> *Write **an** equation and explain what happened.*

Written this way, it now suggests that there are multiple acceptable answers, including the one submitted by my student's sister.

> *Wait! It's more than just coming up with multiple answers!*
> *Well, that's what you said anyway.*

Correct! It's not enough to just come up with multiple answers. They have to be multiple answers that you can prove. In other words, you have to be able to justify them.

> *Write an equation **and** explain what happened.*

Having multiple answers is good, but not if they don't make any sense. Let's look at my student's sister's example again.

Here's her equation:

$$(12|2) - 2 = 4$$

And here's her explanation:

$$12 = \text{total doughnuts}$$
$$2 = \text{total friends}$$
$$12/2 = 6 \text{ for each friend}$$
$$6 - 2 = 4 \text{ (Michael wanted 2 doughnuts too)}$$

Michael had 12 doughnuts, and being the nice person that he is, decided that he wanted to give them to his friends until he remembered that he liked doughnuts too. So, he took two for himself. This was the perfect explanation to justify her equation.

Had her equation been incorrect, or had her explanation been faulty, then marking it wrong would have been justified. But it wasn't.

I never did get around to calling the teacher, so I have no idea what answer she was looking for, but I know that my student's sister's answer shouldn't have been marked wrong.

She needs those points added back to her score! Well, she **should've** had them added back. It's been five years now. Pretty sure she's moved on. But I have had a point to make with this trip down memory lane.

If you recall, Flexible Thinking is the ability to think about things in a new way. (That's "new" to you, by the way. It doesn't have to be unique to anybody else.) If you can look at a problem and remind yourself to come up with multiple potential answers, some you might not have ever considered until that very moment, you're well on your way. After you've come up with the solutions, run them through your "Justify-o-meter" and ask yourself if they make sense. The only person who knows if they make sense is you unless you're not sure, in which case run them through someone else's "Justify-o-meter" and get some feedback.

Remember:

> *There is no such thing as a right or wrong answer.*
> *Simply what you can prove and what you can't.*

And

> *Replace "the" right answer with "a" right answer when attempting to find a solution.*

Imagineer Solutions

Imagineer Solutions

In 1942, Alcoa Aluminum Company took out an ad in Time Magazine that said:

For a long time, we've sought a word to describe what we all work at hard here at Alcoa. IMAGINEERING is the word. Imagineering is letting your imagination soar and then engineering it down to earth.
1942, February 16. Time, 59–59.

Imagineering.

The first time I heard this word was when we took my daughter to Disney World for the first time. My father, ever the curious and enthusiastic student, asked me if I knew what we called the people who created the attractions at Disney World. I did not.

"Imagineers," he proclaimed happily, and I remember thinking what a cool word that was; a melding of the words **imagination** and **engineer**.

My father was, and still is, the King of Imagination as far as I am concerned. When I was a child, he knew how to fan the flames of my creativity, much to my mother's amusement. My mother is an artist in her spare time, so creativity wasn't lost on her, but my dad took using his imagination to a whole new level. One of the stories we both remember fondly is when we went out to dinner and, while waiting for our food, created entire stories about the people who lived in the water droplets in our straws. Then there was the time he came to my First-Grade class and led us on a journey through the imaginary forest, complete with sound effects. I still remember the squeals of excitement that came from my classmates and me when we came across the lions, the tigers, and the bears. (Oh my!)

In addition to his imagination, my father was and still is, a techno-geek. He loves any and everything that deals with technology. If it has a battery or can be plugged in, he wants it, and so do I. We have competitions around who is going to get the newest cell phone first. He used to tell me about how, as a child, he wanted to create motorized roller skates and spent the entire summer trying to figure out what kind of motor he would need. This was in 1958 before the invention of rollerblades and such, but my father has long been endowed with the gift of "What If," and he gave that same gift to me.

See, I was that kid who would try just about anything once so that I could see "what if." While this is great in theory, it also meant I was in trouble. A lot. Like the time I wondered what would happen if I moved that thing next to the driver's seat from **P** to **R** while I was on the incline in our driveway. Or the time I put a piece of paper on the light bulb in my room to see how long it would take to burn. Yeah. Fits. I gave my parents fits.

So, to channel my imagination and my "what-if" inclinations into something that wasn't going to raise their car insurance premiums or burn the house down, my father bought me every science kit he could find. Chemistry, Physics, Biology, electronics, computers, if it involved a problem that needed to be solved, it was at my house.

Picture it, Sicily 1922…

Okay. Not really. But picture it, Newton, Massachusetts 1982.

It's about 9:00 on a Saturday morning, and suddenly a familiar tune breaks the silence.

Dun dun dunnuh dun dun dunnuh dododoooo dododoooo do do

You look over at the chair closest to your bed, and laying across it is a trench coat and a hat, just the right size for a 9-year-old girl. On the table next to the chair is a large envelope and on the front in big red letters are the words TOP SECRET. Inside are your instructions for the day's mission that end with a final warning

This message will self-destruct in three seconds. 3...2...1...

DUN-NUUUUUUH!

(Hopefully, you got my attempt at writing out the theme song to Mission: Impossible)

But this is how Saturday mornings with my Dad went for the better part of my childhood. He'd create problems that needed solving, and I would use whichever handy-dandy science kit was available to solve it. I'd just keep "what-iffing" it until I came up with the solution (or solutions) that worked best. In other words, I imagineered them.

Imagineering is letting your imagination soar and then engineering it down to earth.

Technically, the word "Imagineering" means to create something new that is tangible, so I'm bending the rules just a bit here, but the concept still applies. Dictionary.com defines it as:

The implementing of creative ideas into [sensible] form

In other words, taking those ideas out of our heads and turning them into something practical. And I happen to like this definition because it has a form of my favorite word in it.

Creativity.

Now, if you're one of those people who hear this word and cringe, relax.

I don't have a creative bone in my body!

Maybe not, but you do have a funny one. It's humerus.

Okay. Corny joke. I know, but you don't need to have a creative bone in your body. What you **do** need is to think about creativity the way Author Rudolph Flesch did:

"Creative thinking may simply mean the realization that there is no particular virtue in doing things the way they've always been done."

Are you sensing a pattern here?

Creativity isn't just about being able to sing, dance, paint, sculpt, write, draw, act, or any of a host of other things we tend to think about when we hear the word. It's more than

that. And I submit to you that you do have a creative bone in your body actually, except it's not a bone. It's your brain.

I **could** spend the next few pages peppering you with quotes about creativity and imagination (cuz I got a ton of 'em), but instead, I'm only going to give you my top five favorites. Hopefully, they will ease your mind before I challenge you to put your Imagineering skills to the test. So, here they are:

1) Creativity is intelligence having fun. *Albert Einstein*

2) Creativity is about fresh thinking.

3) Creativity means having an appetite for discovery.

4) Creativity means thinking up new ideas to solve problems.

5) Creativity is the process of having original ideas that have value. *Sir Ken Robinson*

Look at my list carefully, one more time. Do you see anything that requires you to relive your days in elementary school or kindergarten? Any finger painting? Cutting and/or pasting?

Right.

And that's because creativity and imagination stem from what we **think**. Imagineering is about what we **do** with what we thought. So, you ready to give it a try?

But before you do, I want to tell you a quick story.

Long ago, in a galaxy not far away (because it's here), there was a mighty king named Alexander the Great. While on his quest for world domination, he came across the most complicated knot ever known. According to legend, anyone who was able to unwind the knot would conquer all of Asia. Since Alexander was in the business of conquering things and Asia was next on his to-do list, he decided to solve the problem of the knot. After several unsuccessful attempts at unraveling the knot by hand, he decided on a different approach. He took out his sword, sliced the knot in half, and claimed victory.

Do you know why I love this story? Because it's a perfect example of what it means to "implement a creative idea in a practical form." Do you know why the knot was still there when Alexander arrived? Because everyone else was stuck on the idea that the only way to unravel the knot was to do it by hand. In another telling of the story, Alexander is recorded as yelling, "It doesn't matter how the knot is unraveled," right before taking his sword to it. I mean, there was nothing in the "Unravel the Knot" rule book that said it had to be undone by hand. But when you're unfamiliar with flexible thinking or what it means to be an Imagineer, you miss out on opportunities to conquer Asia.

So, you ready?

In our last section, *Allow For Multiple Answers*, we established that looking for **a** right answer instead of **the** right answer opens up the door to many possibilities and helps us practice our flexible thinking skills. However, since we aren't physically in the same place and I can't hear what all of your answers are, I'm going to tell you that there is **technically** one particular answer, but I don't want that to be

the focus here. The focus should be you attempting to come up with as many creative solutions as possible. As a reminder:

There are no right or wrong answers. Simply what you can prove and what you can't.

So again, the only criterium is that your answers must make sense. They must be both plausible and logical. Here's the problem you must solve:

On a warm summer night, the local police department receives an urgent call. Something horrible has happened at a house nearby. When they arrive, they discover Mickey and Minnie dead on the floor, surrounded by glass and water. The only living creature in the house was a cat who they take in for questioning.
How did Mickey and Minnie die?

Remember to "let your imagination soar and then engineer it down to earth." Think of every over the top answer you can come up with and then whittle each one down until you come up with one that fits the criterium. It's all about fresh thinking and new ideas.

Here's another one:

A woman had two sons who were born on the same hour of the same day of the same month of the same year, but they were not twins. **How could this be so?**

So, how'd you do? Imagineer any good ideas? Come up with multiple solutions? How'd it feel? At this point, I can sense your eyes looking at me through the pages of this book. No. I'm not going to tell you what answers I was looking for.

The purpose of these exercises wasn't so you could find **the** answer. It was so you could experience what it feels like to imagineer solutions and come up with **a bunch of** answers. The purpose was for you to practice thinking up new ideas to solve problems and practice flexible thinking.

Congratulations! You're well on your way!

Learn to Take Risks

Learn to Take Risks

Twenty years from now, you will be more disappointed by the things you didn't do than by the ones you did. ---Mark Twain

Some years ago, a story was floating around about a college student who had a fascinating response to a test question. The student was to respond in essay form to the following:

What's the riskiest thing you've ever done?

His response?

This.

Yup. That was his real answer. As a former teacher, I should be annoyed by this. He didn't follow the directions and provide a response in essay form. But I'm not. You know why?

Because he didn't follow the directions and provide a response in essay form.

If you haven't figured it out yet, I have a unique way of looking at things, and I've always been a bit rebellious. I never fit in as a child, so I spent a lot of time channeling my inner Frank Sinatra and doing things my way. Which, I might add, sometimes got me in a whole lot of trouble (Remember, I gave my parents fits?). In my defense, however, I tried to fit in. I tried to follow the rules, but some rules just didn't make sense. Like when your teacher would tell you to do something, and you'd ask them why, and they'd say, "because I said so." Sir and/or ma'am. That is not a sufficient response to my inquiry. Please come back to me when you can answer my question. Yup. I was **that** kid. Or at least I was in my head because had I responded that way, I probably would have gone missing. John and Phyllis, aka Mom and Dad, weren't having it. But as I grew up, I did become **that** adult. And then I became **that** teacher who then taught her students to be **those** people, thus passing on the legacy of children who give their parents fits (My sincerest apologies to all of the parents whose kids I taught).

I believed, and still believe, that nothing is above questioning. My philosophy is:

Question everything but do your research.

But the truth is sometimes just asking a question can be risky, and history is replete with examples of people who did just that. We'll get to a few of them later in this section. But for now, let's discuss what it means to take a risk.

On the previous page, I gave you an example of a student's response, and I told you I wasn't annoyed by it. The reason I wasn't annoyed is because I understood what he was doing. By making the word "this" his whole answer, he both answered the question and provided an example. He responded to the question, "what's the riskiest thing you've ever done" by doing the riskiest thing he'd ever done.

Brilliant, I tell you.

Had he been my student, not only would he have gotten credit for the question, but I might have even given him an extra point or two just for being creative. Now, the next person who tried to answer the question with the same response wouldn't have gotten credit, but that's what happens when you take a risk. The definition itself says as much.

Risk: to do something that may result in a loss, failure, etc.

The keyword here is "may," as in it's possible, this thing you did could result in a loss or failure, but it's not certain, so try it anyway. That's why so many of us are risk-averse. We don't want to do anything that may result in a loss or failure. But what if we applied a little flexible thinking to this definition? Let me offer you an alternative.

*Risk: to do something that may result in a **gain, success**, etc.*

Now, if you try to find my definition of "risk" in the dictionary, you won't because the word is always associated with something negative. Don't believe me? Google "definition of risk" and see what happens. I'll wait.

If you actually took the time to go to Google, you found over 589,000,000 results in 0.74 seconds, and if you went through all 589,000,000 of those results, you found variations of a theme. You also have way too much time on your hands. But the point I'm trying to make is not one of those definitions looks at "risk" as something positive. That's why when people take risks, and they turn out well, we shower them with admiration. They did something we would never do. But perhaps we should.

What the word "risk" needs is a good PR campaign, one that highlights the positive. Kind of like when the National Pork Bureau wanted to extol the nutritional benefits of pork, so they created the "Pork: It's the Other White Meat" slogan. I don't think it would be far-fetched either. I mean, the definitions are just different sides of the same coin. So, if we focused on the positive instead of the negative, people might be more inclined to take leaps of faith.

Leaps of Faith.

Isn't it interesting that when we see this phrase, we don't have any negative feelings? No one has ever used "I'm leap of faith averse" as a reason why they don't want to do something. And yet, taking a "leap of faith" is the exact same thing as taking a risk.

*Leap of Faith: to do something even though **you are not sure** it is right or will succeed.*

That "you are not sure" part means "there's a possibility that," which means "may." Go back to the original definition of risk. It's the same thing.

So, what might "taking a risk" look like in our lives? Well, in my life, taking a risk looked like the first time I posted a picture of myself post-amputation.

Unless you happen to follow me on social media, you probably don't know that since 2018, I am a partial paraplegic and a bilateral lower-limb amputee. What this means is that I now use a wheelchair as my primary source for mobility[3]*, and I am a right-above knee and a left-below knee amputee. The "how" I got to this place is a story for another day (wrote a whole book about it, actually), but when I posted that first picture, I didn't know what was going to happen. Would people shy away from me? Would I become the source of ridicule? Would I lose friends? Terrified doesn't even begin to explain what I felt. But, I took the risk, scared and all, and in a nod to *The Hunger Games*, the odds were in my favor.

One last thing. The reason why most of us don't like to take risks is because it's scary. Fear is the Number One reason why we avoid trying new things. I've never had any desire to skydive because I'm terrified of falling out of a plane (and no, I don't plan on getting over that fear). Likewise, I used to be afraid of speaking in public, but that's a fear I got over. When I had to learn how to drive again, I was scared of getting back behind a car's wheel. Could it have ended in my having a loss or failure? Yes. But because I didn't want to be stuck in the house for the rest of my life, I had to take the risk and confront my fear. Now, I'm rarely home, and I'm back to being stuck in traffic. Oh, the joy.

While in the classroom, I came across many a student who was terrified of public speaking. One young lady, in particular, cried through her first attempt at an oral presentation. Having had the same fear until I got past my

---

[3] By the way, when I say "mobility" I mean how I get around in my house and in my community. It doesn't mean that I don't drive because I do. My car has hand controls that are pretty awesome. Clearly someone with some creativity and flexible thinking came up with this brilliant idea.

freshman year of high school, I told her that I didn't care if she cried on her second attempt, but she was going to complete her presentation even if she had to do it scared. She is now completing her senior year at The University of Georgia, and you want to know what her major is? Broadcast Journalism.

What about you? What might "taking a risk" look like? If you don't know right now, that's okay. The request I'm making may be an easy one in theory but putting it into practice is entirely different. So, I challenge you to do what I asked my student to do, what I tell myself to do every time I expose myself to new environments and new people, fully embracing my new normal. Do It Scared. Here are three examples of people who took risks and reaped positive outcomes to give you some encouragement.

Vivian Malone Jones[4]
On June 11, 1963, Vivian Jones and James Hood became the first Black students to enroll at the University of Alabama. The idea that she wanted to attend was risky enough, but attempting to register was bordering on suicide. Her decision became especially significant when, on the following day, Civil Rights Leader Medgar Evers was murdered in Jackson, MS, for speaking against the South's racial injustices. It would have been understandable had she changed her mind, but instead, she went to class. "I decided not to show any fear and went to classes that day," she said in an interview. In 1965, Jones became the first Black female graduate.

---

[4] 4 Martin, Douglas. "Vivian Malone Jones, 63, Dies; First Black Graduate of University of Alabama." *New York Times*, 14 Oct. 2005,

Vera Wang[5]

Born to Chinese immigrants, Vera Wang was hired as an editor for Vogue Magazine right after graduating from Sarah Lawrence College. At the time, she was the youngest editor at the publication, where she stayed for 17 years before joining Ralph Lauren. Sensing the need to go out on her own, Wang took a considerable risk and, at 40 years of age, walked away from her financially stable career to launch her fashion label. As a result, she is widely regarded as one of the most prestigious fashion designers to come out of the United States, creating gowns for such notable celebrities as Michelle Obama, Alicia Keys, and Kim Kardashian.

Sylvester Stallone[6] In the early 70s, Sylvester Stallone, was a struggling actor in Hollywood, with few options available to him. After going to a Muhammad Ali fight, he wrote the screenplay for *Rocky* in less than four days. When he was able

to present it to producers, they loved it and offered to bring it to the screen. However, he couldn't star in it. Despite his need, he refused to accept any offer that didn't cast him as the lead. As a result, he was offered a much smaller paycheck, but it was a risk worth taking. The Rocky franchise is now worth over $1 billion.

[5] "5 Wildly Successful Entrepreneurs Reveal How Risk Taking Propelled Their Careers." *Inc.*, 3 Oct. 2018, https://www.inc.com/partners-in-leadership/5-wildly-successful-entrepreneurs-reveal-how-risk-taking-propelled-their-careers.html.

[6] Ward, Tom. "The Amazing Story Of The Making Of 'Rocky'." *Forbes*, 29 Aug. 2017, https://www.forbes.com/sites/tomward/2017/08/29/the-amazing-story-of-the-making-of-rocky/#233d7176560b.

Widen Your Perspective

Widen Your Perspectives

When my daughter was younger, we used to go out to eat just about every Saturday morning. Now that she's older, breakfast with OJ has turned into brunch with Bellinis, but it's still one of our favorite ways to spend a Saturday morning. While in the car, my radio was almost always tuned to the local NPR station, and right at the time when we would be either heading to or leaving from, brunch the radio trivia show *Wait, Wait, Don't Tell Me* would come on. Based on the news from the previous week, *Wait Wait* is a funny, cheeky, quirky, less stressful version of *Jeopardy* without the potential for large cash prizes and Alex Trebek. My daughter believed I should've been a contestant because no one knows more useless information than me.

"How do you know that? Better yet, **why** do you know that" she'd often ask.

It's not that the information I have is useless. It's just random. See, I'm an information hoarder.

In my 47 years of living, I have collected more bits and pieces of intellectual minutia than any one human being should be allowed to have. Want to win Trivia Night at the local Applebees? Hit me up. But it's not just that I like trivia. I like learning. If someone would pay me a six or seven-figure salary to be a full-time student, I would. My husband says that cable is completely wasted because I only like to watch four or five channels: The Smithsonian Channel, The History Channel, The Science Channel, The Travel Channel, and PBS.

If it wasn't for him, I'd never have known about the televised gems that are *Sanford and Son, Family Guy,* and *Curb Your Enthusiasm,* and I surely would never have binged watched the first seven seasons of *Game of Thrones* before shaking my fist angrily at Season Eight (Winter came and I was NOT happy). He keeps me balanced. But for every quirk I have, I blame my parents. My focus on learning comes from them.

Growing up, my hobby was reading, and our house was full of all types of books and magazines for me to explore. My mother's hobby was art, so Bob Ross and I spent endless hours painting happy little clouds and trees. My father's hobby was playing the trumpet, so I was exposed to classical, blues, and jazz from an early age. Friday nights were spent playing Scrabble, and Saturday mornings were spent cleaning the house and listening to old Motown music. I played the flute and took Tae Kwon Do lessons. I studied French and tried to learn Swahili, and during my senior year of high school, I learned Russian and added Japanese when I got to college. I found out what happened long ago and in a galaxy far, far away, and I dared to go where no man had gone before. If there was something I didn't know, you could bet your lightsaber I was going to find it out. And because I was a shy only child without a lot of friends, I had plenty of time to add to my treasure chest of knowledge. And I loved every minute of it.

The only thing I loved more than learning was traveling, and I have my parents to thank for that too. Have you ever seen someone share one of those "Let's Get to Know Each Other" posts on Facebook? You know, the ones that ask you to check off all the places you've visited. It usually starts by saying something like, "The average number of places visited is eight" (followed by the shocked face emoji). I loved these because, courtesy of my mom, I've been to more than a few.

My mother gets all the credit for my healthy dose of wanderlust. Growing up on the east side of Cleveland, OH, she always had dreams of traveling, so after she got married, had me, and I was old enough to fly, we were on a flight to Florida. My father was a homebody, so he wasn't interested in going anywhere, but if you know my mother at all, then you know what Phyllis wants, Phyllis gets. So, we traveled.

First, it was Florida, and then it was Puerto Rico. Then we visited every state in New England and every island in The Bahamas. Then we went to most of the islands in the Caribbean, followed by California, Oahu, and Maui. Whenever there was an opportunity to travel on any school trip, she was the first to sign me up. I took my first trip out of the country without my parents to Quebec when I was in the 8th grade and then traveled to Washington D.C., London, Moscow, and St. Petersburg when I was in high school. But make no mistake. My mother's desire to travel was more than just the fulfillment of her bucket list. My mother was laser-focused on one thing for me.

Exposure.

When it comes to widening or expanding our perspectives, it can't be done if we don't ever see, do, or learn anything new. My mother was keenly aware that if I was to be successful in any capacity, I had to be exposed to things other than what I had access to in my hometown. That's why I know so much "useless information." She wanted to make sure that I could hold my own in various areas and in a variety of situations.

The most common definition for **perspective** is,

a particular attitude toward or way of regarding something; a point of view.

How our perspectives are shaped is solely based on our experiences or by what we are exposed to.

Your reality is as you perceive it to be. So, it is true that by altering this perception, we can alter our reality.
William Constantine

Right now, in 2020, The United States of America is anything but. Everything from politics and religion to sports and entertainment has us at odds with each other and pretty much the world. Every day it seems like someone is mad at someone else for something they disagree with. It's exhausting. And the truth is it would be much easier for us to be more united if everyone was willing to alter their perspectives ever so slightly.

I'm not saying we should agree with ideas that are fundamentally against who we are at our core, but how different would our country be if we were to simply say, "I respect your viewpoint, but I don't agree." How different would **we**, as individuals, be?

Widening our perspectives isn't about forcing anyone to change their minds. It's about us being open to respecting viewpoints that are different than our own. The adage, "don't judge a man until you've walked a mile in his shoes," still has value. I've also heard someone put it this way,

Don't judge me for the choices I make when you don't know the options I had to choose from.

All in all, this next step in our journey of flexible thinking is dependent upon or willingness to do something differently, to expose ourselves to ideas, concepts, people, places, and things that are outside of our usual. This isn't just useful in our personal lives. It can be helpful in our entrepreneurial lives too. Go back and look at the previous four sections we've discussed. Is it possible that expanding our perspectives could help us? Is it possible that broadening our perspectives could help us Slay the Sacred Cow, Allow for Multiple Answers, Imagineer Solutions, and Learn to Take Risks?

Of course, it can.

But if this is a problematic idea for you to grab hold of, here are a few small steps you can try. And don't worry. Small steps are still steps, and little progress is still progress. As a former runner, we had a saying: "Your race. Your pace. A mile is still a mile whether you run it in eight minutes or 15." So, take your time. You'll get there when you're ready.

The To-Do List

Five Ways to Widen Your Perspective

1) **Travel:** This doesn't have to be a long distance away from home (although traveling to other countries is a great way to expand your perspective). It can be to another city, state, or region. Just make it somewhere different than what you're used to

2) **Try New Foods:** You may not be able to travel to other countries, but you can certainly eat from other countries. Choose a restaurant that serves food from someplace you'd like to travel and go there. If that's too adventurous for you, simply try eating foods from other regions or cultures in the United States. I am from Massachusetts, and one of my favorite sandwiches is called a "Fluffernutter," which is marshmallow spread and peanut butter on white bread. Hey. Don't knock it until you've tried it!

3) **Learn A New Language:** Another great way to increase your exposure is to learn another language. Did you know that most of the world is bilingual? It's actually a requirement for students to graduate in many countries, knowing more than one language fluently. To start, you can learn Spanish or French. The languages have many similarities, and I've been told that learning one is much more comfortable if you know the other.

4) **Listen to New Music:** At home, I was exposed to jazz, blues, classical, and the Motown Sound. At school, I

was exposed to rap, hip-hop, R&B, rock, heavy metal, and pop. When I went to college, it was reggae, calypso, House, and Go-Go, and when I moved down South, I learned all about Country and its variations. One of my former students is into K-Pop, and she swears I have not lived until I've listened to it, so I guess I'll add that to my list.

5) **Watch a Movie:** This may seem like a simple task, but there are lots of movies out that may be different than what you're used to watching. If you're not into superhero movies, might I suggest making your way through the MCU (Marvel Cinematic Universe)? If musicals aren't your thing, *Mary Poppins* (the new one or the old one) is a safe bet along with *The Greatest Showman* and *Dreamgirls*. Don't like romances? Try *50 First Dates* or *The Notebook*. Regardless, try watching something that is the opposite of your usual and expand your horizons!

nterrupt the Idea

Interrupt the Idea

I like sports. I was a sprinter in high school and became a long-distance runner as an adult, having completed 5Ks, 10Ks, and a few half-marathons. I love watching tennis, gymnastics, soccer, baseball, basketball, golf, volleyball, boxing, and hockey. Most of these I learned to love by cheering on my students. But my favorite sport, hands down, is football. I was raised on it, and according to my father, I was a fan before I was even born.

The story goes that on Christmas Eve 1972, my father was watching the Cleveland Browns play the Miami Dolphins when my mother started having contractions. My father was engrossed in the game when she announced it was time for her to go to the hospital. This was a pivotal game for the Browns, and every one of their fans, because they were in the playoffs. But my father, excited about becoming a dad, did what any loving husband would do. He leaned over to my mother's stomach and asked me not to come until after the game was over. And you know what happened next? My mother's contractions stopped, and I wasn't born until the next day.

On Christmas.

Not only was my mother incredulous about my father's behavior, but she's also spent the last 47 years reminding me that because I sided with my father and didn't come until Christmas Day, she missed out on dinner at my aunt's house.

And she wasn't able to eat until December 26 because, by the time I arrived, the hospital's kitchen was closed. Oops.

So, I grew up loving football. I don't have a team per se, but I tend to follow players, especially those I know personally, because they graduated from the school where I used to teach. And I raised my daughter to love football too.

If you've ever been a fan of the early seasons of *The Cosby Show*, then you'll recall an episode when little Rudy Huxtable decided that she wanted to play football. Clair, her mom, was scared she would get hurt until Rudy led her team to victory after being given the nickname "Sweet Feet." My daughter, around the same age in real life as Rudy was on the show, proudly announced one day that not only did she want to play football, but she wanted to be the quarterback. Like Clair, I looked at my sweet little girl and said,

"You know, quarterbacks get sacked a lot. What if you get hurt?"

She looked me in the eyes with the most severe look on her face and said,

"Quarterbacks only get sacked when they get caught, Mommy. They won't catch me."

Insert stunned emoji face here

I never did allow her to play, but she made up for what she couldn't do on a field by watching the games on tv and running around the living room, avoiding imaginary

defensive linemen. She even started tackling pillows, and when I told her that quarterbacks don't tackle anybody, she said,

"I know. I'm doing something different."

Well, alrighty then.

When she got older, her attention switched from pro football to college football, so we'd watch the college games on Saturdays. When it was time for her to choose a college to attend, she had three criteria: 1) It had to be a Division 1 school, 2) It had to be an SEC Division 1 school, and 3) It had to have her major.

Yes. Football came before her college major.

Of course, it couldn't be just any D-1 SEC school. Nope. It had to be LSU, much to my husband's disappointment, the die-hard Georgia Bulldogs fan. It didn't help that at one time, one of my former students played for Auburn, and another played for Alabama, so at any given point in our house, you could hear a "Go Dawgs" a "Roll Tide," a "War Eagle," or a "Geaux Tigers." It was stressful.

One of the best parts of football is when the game is on the line and its 3rd Down and goal. The quarterback has to make something significant happen so his team can win. He calls the play, and the center hikes him the ball. The quarterback catches it and falls back, looking for a receiver in the end zone. Seeing no one open, he calls an audible and charges forward, taking the ball into the endzone himself.

TOUCHDOWN!

Cue touchdown dance

So, what does any of this have to do with interrupting the idea? What is Flexible Thinking again?

The brain's ability to shift from one concept to another.

Interrupting the initial idea for another idea is what you do when you're thinking flexibly. And when a quarterback calls an audible, this is what he's doing (well, that's what the good ones are doing anyway).

Now, I could just end the book right here and go off and watch a few playoff games (it's the end of football season right now), but shifting from one concept to another isn't necessarily as simple as it sounds. Let me give you an everyday scenario.

Your friend invites you to lunch at noon. When you put the location into your GPS, you realize you've been to the restaurant before, so you hop in your car and go. Along the way, you run into traffic. The GPS tells you to take an alternate route, but because you've been to the restaurant before and don't recognize the new directions, you ignore the GPS and continue.

Rerouting...

The GPS chooses a different route to help you get out of the traffic you're stuck in, but again, because you've been to the restaurant before and don't know the new route, you

ignore it. Besides, you're not too far away from your destination.

Rerouting...

Again, the GPS tries to send you in a different direction to avoid the traffic, but you're so close to the restaurant, and the new route is still unfamiliar, so you once again ignore the alternate directions. Now you find yourself gridlocked, two blocks from the restaurant. Looking ahead, you notice that cars coming from the opposite direction are moving freely, and you can see people turning into the restaurant where you're supposed to be. Suddenly it occurs to you that had you listened to your GPS, you'd be seated at the restaurant enjoying a drink and a good meal with a friend.

I know I'm not the only one who's done this before. We get so comfortable doing what we've always done that even when we see a situation that we need to avoid or adjust, we don't. Why? Because it's challenging to shift to something we don't already know.

In our traffic example, we were given multiple opportunities to do something differently, to shift our thinking from one idea to another. But, because we didn't know any of the alternate routes, we stayed stuck in traffic and missed our lunch. Had we known any of the alternate routes, we would have had no problem shifting our thinking. It's the unknown that keeps us stuck.

Now, back to my football example. When a quarterback calls an audible, he's not shifting to a play he doesn't know. A

quarterback has a playbook and in that playbook are a bunch of potential plays he can choose from. But even if what he decides isn't **in** the playbook, it's still not unfamiliar to him because (hopefully) he's been playing long enough to have a few extra plays up his sleeve.

When I work with teachers, I observe them in their rooms while class is in session. As they're delivering their lesson, sometimes things don't go according to plan, and they are faced with one of two choices: A) continue with the lesson or B) call an audible. When experienced teachers call an audible, they aren't pulling a lesson out of thin air no matter what it looks like. It might not be written down, but they are drawing on an entire knowledge set gained through their experience as teachers. Their initial thought of "hey, here's how this lesson is going to go" shifts to "hey, here's how this lesson is going to go **now**." The goal has not changed. It's **how to accomplish the goal** that has changed. They've shifted their thoughts from "what was" to "what now is." They've interrupted their original idea for something else.

So, what does this look like in our day-to-day lives? How can we practice calling audibles? One way is to deliberately put ourselves in situations that require us to think on our feet, which, by the way, is another example of what it means to interrupt one idea to shift to another. Try learning a strategy game like chess or checkers or if you're into video games, choose one that is similar to the one you already know how to play but offers a more significant challenge.

When faced with a difficult situation, stop and think of all the ways you **could** respond and then **choose** to respond differently. When I became an amputee and found myself confined to a wheelchair. There are a whole lot of responses I could, and did, have. Most of them weren't very productive and involved me doing a lot of crying and cursing. But neither of those responses was doing anything to help me get back to the business of living. So, I had to shift my thinking from what I could no longer do to what I could still do and then to what **else** I could do. I can no longer go for a run, but I can even get out of the house and be mobile, **and** I can move faster on wheels than I ever could with legs.

Is any of this easy? Nope. But it's also not impossible. It **can** be done if you're willing to call an audible.

Neutralize the Negative

Neutralize Your Negative Words and Thoughts

In the section **Widen Your Perspective**, I let you know that I don't watch a lot of television. If not for my husband and his eclectic taste in shows, there's quite a few I would know nothing about. What I **do** watch a lot of is movies. I don't make it to the movie theatre, but when you have Netflix, Hulu, and now Disney+, who needs to leave the house? What I lack in tv show variety I more than makeup for with my movie picks. But my favorite movies are the ones that are supposed to be reserved for kids. Movies like *Shrek 1, 2, and 3, The Incredibles 1 and 2,* all the iterations of *Toy Story, Monsters, Inc, Beauty and the Beast, Zootopia, Up,* and *Finding Nemo* are among my favorites. I actually took myself to see *Finding Dory* and sat next to a 5-year-old who passed me a tissue when my eyes started leaking after Dory found her family. I can recite every word in *Aladdin,* and you probably don't want to be seated next to me if you'll have an issue with me singing every song in *The Lion King.* But one of my favorite movies is both simple enough for kids to relate to and sophisticated enough for adults to question why it wasn't made for **us** sooner.

Inside Out is about a girl named Riley who finds herself uprooted from a quiet town in Minnesota to an unfamiliar and decidedly larger, San Francisco. As her family begins to settle in, Riley finds herself in an all-out war with her emotions. Joy, Fear, Anger, Disgust, and Sadness all live in the control area of her brain called Headquarters and are at odds with each other over how best to navigate a new city, a new house, and a new school.

As the movie progresses, Riley finds herself trying to navigate some pretty heavy thoughts for an 11-year old as her emotions fight for dominance. Joy tells her to "think positive" while Anger asks, "Can I say the cursed words now?" Sadness suggests, "we could cry until we can't breathe" at the same time as Fear comments, "Alright. We didn't die today. I call that an unqualified success." Disgust, the emotion that seems to be at the core of every pre-teen known to man, is simply irritated by everything and everybody and declares that the family's new home is "the worst place I've been in my entire life." Riley has A LOT going on. And yet, the most pivotal quote in the entire movie comes at the very beginning:

Do you ever look at someone and wonder what is going on inside their head?

The truth is Riley is no different than most of us. When faced with circumstances out of our control, we usually find ourselves in an all-out war, wandering through every emotion and held captive by our thoughts as we try to make sense of it all. For example, someone gains access to your bank account and steals all of your money. What's your first response? If you're thinking logically, you contact the bank, let them know what happened, and they fix it. But how many of us would be thinking logically in a situation like this? Well, that's what happened to me a few months ago, and my first response was to tap Anger on the shoulder and permit him to say all of the cursed words. It wasn't until after I'd spent some time wallowing with Sadness and Disgust that I looked over at Joy, who reminded me that the bank had canceled my card, issued me a new one, apologized for the

inconvenience, and credited my account. But it took A LOT of cursed words before I got to that point, and folks, it wasn't easy.

When we allow our emotions to take over, we permit them to hijack our thoughts, resulting in consequences. In a recent Forbes Magazine article titled "When You Talk to Yourself It Matters: How to Master Your Self Talk," author Jessica Lutz says,

> *"The words we use to speak to ourselves can have a huge impact on us…. Self-talk can have a big impact on your success."*

It can also have a significant impact on what we think. So, if the words we say to ourselves turn into the thoughts we think to ourselves, how we manage what we say and think are vitally important, especially if we're trying to practice flexible thinking.

There's a saying that goes, "we have what we speak." This statement means we can influence what manifests in our lives by merely regulating what comes out of our mouths and, theoretically, in our minds. The 14th-century Persian poet Hafiz puts it like this:

> *The words you speak become the house you live in.*

This is a powerful visual. Imagine that each word we speak or think is a brick that creates our reality. If we speak or think positively, we can find the good in our lives. If we speak or think negatively, well, you get the point. If we want to live

more resilient and happy lives, we have to neutralize every word or thought that is not serving us positively.

Neutralize: *to make (something) ineffective; counteract; nullify.*

This task is not as easy to do as it sounds because many of us are used to speaking and/or thinking negatively about ourselves. And by "many of us," the "us" I am generally referring to is women.

Steps on proverbial soapbox and grabs microphone

There is significant evidence that women are more likely to engage in it than men when it comes to negative self-talk. Some say that this is due to what is called "The Confidence Gap," a theory that suggests women are less self-assured than men. Men tend to be overly confident (or at least they put on the persona of being so), while women tend to be the opposite, but not because they are less secure. It's because a woman's confidence is often misinterpreted as arrogance, which, unlike for men, is perceived as a negative, so we hide it. The confident woman is portrayed as an itch with a "B" added to the front, causing unnecessary issues, especially in the workplace. But, I think that a lot of negative self-talk comes from a different theory altogether for both women and men.

Steps off soapbox and drops mic

The Harvard Business Review defines imposter Syndrome as "a collection of inadequacy feelings that persist despite evident success." "Imposters" are plagued with self-doubt and believe that any success they may have is due more

to luck or chance and less because they earned it. When I was in the classroom, I taught at a predominately Black Magnet high school with a well-respected math/science program. Students who graduated from the program often went on to top colleges and universities across the country. One of my students, in particular, struggled with Imposter Syndrome the entire time he was in high school. He earned straight A's in every class every year, scored a 35/36 on his ACT, 1550 on his SAT, and received a full scholarship to an Ivy League School. And yet…

Today, he is completing his senior year. He has done such notable things as interning for Microsoft and Google and presenting his summer research on pancreatic cancer at an NIH (National Institute of Health) summer conference. I **still** find myself having to convince him that all of his accomplishments aren't flukes. Our next conversation will be all about how to improve his flexible thinking.

Counteracting our negative thoughts and words requires deliberate action. It takes work, and if we've been speaking ill of ourselves for a while, it takes time. Here are a few ways we can practice neutralizing our negative thoughts and words:

The To-Do List

1) **Question What We Think and Say:** When that first negative thought rears its ugly head, we must ask ourselves if it follows the **THINK** rule, which says:
   Is it True?
   Is it Helpful

   Is it Inspiring?
   Is it Necessary?
   Is it Kind?

   This strategy is used with children in elementary school when interacting with their peers, but it works just as well when interacting with ourselves. If we can't answer in the affirmative to every one of these questions, we need to dismiss it and move on.

2) **Let It Go:** If you need to channel your inner Elsa for this one, feel free. But if our thoughts and words aren't working in concert to bring about a positive outcome, we don't need to dwell on them. We need to let them go.

3) **Check Yourself Before You Wreck Yourself:** (Shout out to Ice Cube). If we understand that our words and thoughts can either build us up or tear us down, we need to put them in check. In other words, we need to be aware of what we think and say about ourselves and only accept the things that we want to use to"build the house we live in."

4) **Just Say "No":** As we begin to put our flexible thinking skills into practice, we need to learn to say "no" to those negative thoughts when they creep upon us. There's a cartoon that I often use that shows a series of frames of a

woman repeatedly saying "no" to whatever is on her computer screen. When my thoughts start to get away from me, I say "no" out loud repeatedly until they pass.

5) **Write and Throw:** This is just what it sounds like. When negative thoughts start to overwhelm you, write

them down and then throw them away. You can even go so far as to write them down and burn them. The key is that by destroying the thoughts on paper, you are practicing destroying them in your mind.

Destroy the Box

Destroy the Box

Boxes are designed to do one of two things: Keep things out or keep things in. They are a form of protection. But they can also be a source of extreme frustration, especially when you want out what's in the box. I was born on Christmas, so as a kid, this was obviously my favorite day of the year. No. I didn't get combination gifts. My mother wasn't having that. I got Christmas gifts **and** birthday gifts, and she made sure I knew which was which by signing all of my Christmas gifts "From Santa" and all my birthday gifts "Love Mom & Dad." And yes, she still does (Thanks, Mom).

One Christmas, when I turned seven, I woke up early at my grandparents' house to find my grandfather in the place where he spent most of his time sitting in front of his CB radio. In the 21st Century, the idea of a CB seems archaic, but when I was a child, this is how my grandfather connected with people all over the country. Unless you're a truck driver or over 40, you probably have no idea what a CB radio is. "CB" stands for "Citizen Band, and it's a range of radio frequencies that any of us is allowed to use. While they aren't often used for personal use anymore, emergency responders use them all the time, especially when specific infrastructure isn't available during disasters.

But there he was, sending Christmas greetings to all of his buddies who were doing the same thing as he was that morning. When I rounded the corner, his face lit up, and he said, "Good Morning Christmas Baby!" I skipped over to him in my footie pajamas and got ready for our annual ritual. My grandfather sat me in his lap and grabbed the handset. "Breaker, Breaker 1-9, this is Big John coming from the Buckeye State, and I want to wish y'all a Merry Christmas, so y'all can wish my grandbaby a happy birthday!"

Or something like that…

Almost instantly, birthday greetings started pouring in from all over the country. There were even a few from people who had been keeping track of my birthdays for some years because they knew how old I was without my grandfather having to tell them. I loved these moments.

After we did this for almost an hour, I went over to look at all the gifts that were under the tree. I picked out the ones that were mine and stacked them neatly together, so, you know, I could be efficient when it was time to open gifts with the rest of the family. As I placed each one in a pile, I tried to guess what it was. I squished every package and shook every box, and then did my best to be patient. I didn't know what time it was, but it sure took a long time for the rest of the house to get up.

I remember sitting on the floor next to my stack and pouting. I looked up at my grandfather, who had been watching me organize my gifts. He smiled.

"So, you ready to open up your gifts, huh?" I shook my head, "yes."

"Well, which would do you want to open first?" I pointed to a medium-sized box, still pouting. My grandfather laughed.

"I don't know what you're pouting for. Gone ahead and open it!"

At this point in my story, I feel I should mention that I was not aware of the Christmas Day rule that said, "children are to wait until their parents are in the room before opening any and all gifts." I was seven. And it was Christmas. And did I mention I was seven? But, on that day, my grandfather either didn't know the Christmas Day rule or he didn't care because by the time my parents and grandmother finally arrived, there was paper scattered everywhere, and I was trying to get into the box that held my newest Barbie doll. I'm sure you're not surprised when I tell you that it didn't go over very well.

While my mother yelled at my grandfather and my father tried to keep my mother from yelling at my grandfather, my grandmother retreated to the kitchen to start breakfast, and I kept trying to get to my Barbie. To this day, I have no idea what they seal those boxes with because if you don't have a chainsaw or a switchblade, it's not happening.

After spending several minutes trying to tear open the box, oblivious to my mother's meltdown, I finally went to my grandfather, held up the box to him, and asked him to open it. Without missing a beat, he pulled out his pocketknife, sliced open the top of the box, and handed it back to me. Suffice it to say, whatever progress my father had made calming my mother down disintegrated as I went back to my pile of unwrapped gifts and tried to open another box.

To be honest, I don't even remember what was in the other boxes. I'd spent so much time and effort trying to get what was **in** the box **out** that the Barbie is the only gift I remember from that day. But when I became a teacher, the concept of getting things out of boxes took on an entirely different meaning.

I began this section by saying that boxes are designed to do one thing: Keep things out or keep things in. Because I taught 9th grade English, I spent a lot of time trying to get students out of their boxes. Of course, I'm not talking about physical boxes (although shipping a few classes off to Siberia did cross my mind once or twice). I'm talking about mental ones.

Ninth graders come to high school around the ages of 13 and 14, and I have to be honest, they aren't the most stable group. If you've ever had the pleasure of having one in your house, then you already know what I mean. Between the mood swings, apathy, forgetfulness, and questionable body odor, this age group is going through what can best be described as an "emotional crucible."

In the book *Primal Teen: What New Discoveries About the Teenage Brain Tell Us About Our Kids*, author Barbara Strauch says that neuroscientists have uncovered clues that suggest, "…the teenage brain may, in fact, be briefly insane." (Come on. You know you've thought it even if you've never actually said it out loud.) The reason stems from the way our brains develop. Did you know that the prefrontal cortex, the part that controls our working memory, inhibition, and impulse

control, doesn't fully develop until we're around 25 years old? So, when teenagers exhibit behavior that makes absolutely no sense, it's because, technically, they don't have any. And when students begin high school, they are usually in the precarious position of being stretched between who they **want** to be and who they think they **have** to be. And this is where those mental boxes come in.

From the moment he arrived at school, "Texas" was ready to fight. The chip on his shoulder was as big as his nickname, and he came in the door, having something to prove. I didn't even know he was still enrolled for the first six weeks of the semester because I'd never seen him. As soon as he finished with one suspension, he was being handed another, and when he finally started coming to my class, he refused to participate. It took a little coercing and a lot of encouragement to get him to the point where he became interested in my class. But when he did, he was one of my best. He very quickly became one of my favorite students, and we are still close. One day, I asked him why his first semester of high school was so difficult, and he said,

"I've been told my whole life that I was going to either end up in jail or the morgue. Until you, no one had told me I could be anything different, so that's what I believed." I wanted to cry and rage at the same time.

In another instance, I had a student who was convinced that he wasn't as smart as his peers. On the one hand, this was a ridiculous assumption (and a fine example of the Imposter Syndrome we talked about in the last section), but on the other hand, I understood why he might have felt this way. His peer group was genuinely extraordinary. Two of his friends would eventually become the valedictorian and the salutatorian of their graduating class, and the rest of them would receive some type of academic scholarship to attend college. The adage that says we are the sum total of the people we spend the most time with meant nothing to him, and I spent the better part of his high school career reassuring him that he wasn't the "weak link." It wasn't until he went to college (on a full scholarship, I might add) that he finally broke out of the box of insecurity and doubt, and now he's one of the go-to leaders on campus.

Getting things out of boxes can be challenging. Getting **people** out of boxes is considerably more difficult. Remember, boxes are a type of protection? Sometimes we stay in our boxes because it's safe. We get comfortable within the walls of the "house we built for ourselves" and prefer to stay there because we don't want to risk what may happen if we don't. For example, people who are introverts tend to shy away from others and avoid large crowds. As an ambivert (someone who has characteristics of both introverts and extroverts), I completely understand the need to keep people out of your space sometimes. I may have previously mentioned that I am an only child who grew up awkwardly shy, so I had a deep fondness for being alone. Honestly, I still do. It's my box, so stay out of it. And yet, had I never ventured outside of my walls of comfort, I would have never discovered that I have a pretty awesome gift for public speaking. It took my thinking outside the box for me to figure that out.

"Think Outside the Box" is a phrase most of us are familiar with. It means to think creatively, unencumbered, or unbothered by rules or restraints. But I have to confess that I hate this phrase. It's been so overused that it's become more of a catchphrase than anything else. The origin, incidentally, comes from this nine-dot puzzle that most of us already know. If you're not, here are the rules:

Using only four lines, connect all the dots without lifting your pen or pencil from the paper.

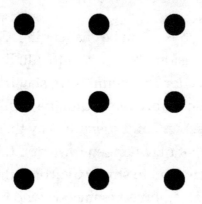

Since I'm not sure if you have ever tried this, I'll leave the answer for you at the end of this section (or you can just Google it. Your choice.). But the clue to solving this is you have to think **outside** the box (Hint, hint) literally. And the reason why many of us can't solve this without Google is that we allow ourselves to be restricted by our thoughts.

I submit that "thinking outside the box" is less about being creative and more about not allowing ourselves to be held captive by what we think. So, with that in mind, let me present to you the DCV (Dr. Chantrise Version) definition of this phrase:

Get Out of Your Head and Destroy the Box.

The "get out of your own head" part is mine. The "destroy the box" part is my dad's. He's never been a box kinda guy, and throughout his career, he's spent a lot of time breaking out of the ones people have tried to put him in. His philosophy is this:

*You don't need to get **out** of a box if you don't allow yourself to get **in** one in the first place.*

If you've got nothing else out of this book, I hope it's that our ability to have both resiliency and flexible thinking comes from our willingness to change the way we think. No one can make us do it, and no one can tell us how long it should take. This is a journey unique to each of us, but until we decide to take control of where this journey takes us, we're going to be stuck right where we are. Don't get stuck. Choose today to grab your R.A.F.T. and go. You still have time.

The Extra Stuff

1) Below are two solutions to the nine-dot puzzle:

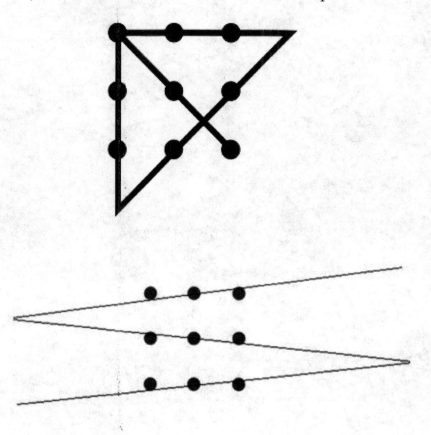

2) Here are the answers to the questions from the **Imagineer Solutions** section (You're welcome).

On a warm summer night, the local police department receives an urgent call. Something horrible has happened at a house nearby. When they arrive, they discover Mickey and Minnie dead on the floor, surrounded by glass and water. The only living creature in the house was a cat who they take in for questioning. **How did Mickey and Minnie die?**

Answer: Mickey and Minnie are fish. The cat knocked over their fishbowl.

*A woman had two sons who were born on the same hour of the same day of the same month of the same year, but they were not twins. **How could this be so?***

Answer: Because they're triplets.

Hey! Thanks for purchasing this book. It's taken me a whole year plus to get it right and just as I was finishing, I came up with yet another idea. Coming soon to an online platform near you:

The Noah Had an Ark. You Need a RAFT
Workbook and Journal

You already know I'm an educator so you also **had** to know this was coming. Well, it's still in the works but if you want to be the first to know when it's available, go to this link: https://bit.ly/RandWSignUp and enter your information. Not only will you get the deets on the workbook's release, but you'll also get **10%** off the price and first dibs on the courses, journals, and merchandise I've been cooking up.

Also, if you're on social media and need someone else to follow, you can find me on Facebook as Chantrise Holliman (personal page), Dr. Chantrise Sims Holliman (business page), Resilient & Winning (Facebook Group).

If IG and Twitter are more your speed, you can follow me on both platforms at @DrChantrise. If you're looking for a professional connection, you can check me out on LinkedIn at Chantrise Sims Holliman, EdD. Want to send an email? Go ahead! Chantrise@DrChantrise.com.

Dr. Chantrise

9 780998 621944